T0130384

AuthorHouse™
1663 Liberty Drive
Bloomington, IN 47403
www.authorhouse.com
Phone: 833-262-8899

Because of the dynamic nature of the Internet, any web addresses or links contained in this book may have changed since publication and may no longer be valid. The views expressed in this work are solely those of the author and do not necessarily reflect the views of the publisher, and the publisher hereby disclaims any responsibility for them.

Any people depicted in stock imagery provided by Getty Images are models, and such images are being used for illustrative purposes only.
Certain stock imagery © Getty Images.

This book is printed on acid-free paper.

ISBN: 978-1-6655-3529-8 (sc)
ISBN: 978-1-6655-3530-4 (e)

Library of Congress Control Number: 2021916937

Print information available on the last page.

Published by AuthorHouse 07/18/2021

authorHOUSE®

THE SLEEPY TOWN PONY

BY: Sharon Hernandez

"Oh, children it's bedtime."

"Yes grandmother." The children came running into the bedroom, and jumped into their beds. Lay down, get comfortable, and go to sleep. The grandmother pulled the blankets upon the children. Sara looked up at her grandmother.

"Please tell us a story", Sara asked.

"Ok, let me see, have I told you two about Sleepy and his town?"

"No grandmother, who is Sleepy and where is his town?" Asked Billy. Looking at his grandmother.

"Where is his town grandmother?" Sara looked at her. The grandmother set down on Sara's bed.

"Well dear let me tell you. It's not far, he lives in Sleepy Town."

"Where is it grandmother?" asked Sara.

"Now, I will tell you about Sleepy, the pony and his town." The children looked at their grandmother with eyes open wide.

"Let me start at the beginning. Well when I was your age, my grandmother told me about Sleepy the pony and Sleepy Town. Sleepy the pony is a very special friend to all children. Sleepy Town is a magical place."

Billy looked at his grandmother. "What do you mean?"

"You will see soon children. He is a little black pony with a star on his forehead. He lives in sleepy Town. Grandmother said. "His name is Sleepy is the town named after him."

"Sleepy will be coming soon to take you two with him to his home for a visit." The Grandmother looked down at the face of the children.

"Grandmother, I don't want to go to Sleepy Town. I have to stay here with you Grandmother."

"He will come for Sara and you."

"Billy, you will have so much fun, I did when I was there. I missed seeing my good friend Sleepy. When I was, your age went to Sleepy Town all the time. I remember so many good times."

"So when is he coming to get us?" Billy asked.

"He will come for you two soon and take you to Sleepy Town. He will come for you in your dreams to pick you up." Billy looked at his grandmother.

"You will climb on his back, and away you two will ride to Sleepy Town. You will play games and eat sweet food. And when it's time for you to come home, he will bring you two home again."

The Grandmother looked down at the children. They were fast asleep. She bent over, and kissed their foreheads.

"Sweet dreams my little darling. O.k. Sleepy, they are all yours now. Please, take care of my grandchildren."

Just then, Billy and Sara heard a voice.

"Hey Billy, Sara are you ready?" The children set up in their beds. There was a little black pony standing in their bedroom. Billy and Sara looked at the pony.

"How did you get in here?" Billy asked.

"I go anywhere I want to see my friends."

"You talk!" Billy said.

"Yes, your grandmother didn't tell you two I talk? All of us ponies in Sleepy Town talk."

Sara looked at the pony.

"I'm your friend, so climb on my back and we will go."

"Where to?" Billy asked.

"To Sleepy Town of course." said the pony.

"Your grandmother is a good friend of mine."

Billy looked at the pony. "But ponies don't talk."

"Your grandmother told you I was a special pony. So now, it's time to go. "Said the pony.

The children climbed on the pony's back.

"Hold on children", said the pony. Just then, the closet door opened, and the pony walked in to it. And the closet door closed behind them. Then the children looked around and saw Sunshine, rainbows, gumdrop trees, lollipop flowers, and cotton candy bushes. The biggest play ground with swings merry—go—rounds, slides and pony rides.

And club house's all in a roll. Girls on one side and boys is on the other side. There was all of Billy and Sara's friends from the past, present and the future. All the children were playing and visiting with all their friends. Sara's and her friends have tea parties, Billy and his friend's play baseball and football.

The boy's and girl's played all kinds of games. They took turns riding the ponies. Some of the ponies moons, suns, stripes or stars in their foreheads. And all the ponies talked. The children had fun riding the ponies around the playground.

They stopped to have a picnic lunch and went back to playing for hours. Billy and Sara were so happy to play with their friends.

Then the pony Sleepy said to Billy and Sara, "It is time to go home." The children climb on the pony's back, and the way they rode off to take them home. Billy and Sara wake up in their beds. They look at each other.

"Sara are you tired?" ask Billy.
"No, Billy are you?"
"No Sara," said Billy.
Just then, they heard their grandmother say, "breakfast in 15 minutes you two. Are you two ready for school?"

"In a minute grandmother." The children looked at each other.
"Do you remember Sleepy?" asked Sara.
"Yes, but I thought I was dreaming Sara?" said Billy.
"Me too, but he is real Billy," said Sara. Looking at Billy.

Their grandmother walked in to the room.
"You two need to get ready for school. Now get ready for school."

"Ok grandmother", said the children. They eat they breakfast and out the door to school. They walk in to the school all they friends was there. Their friends ran to Sara and Billy.

"Do you remember last night?" One of Billy friends ask him, it was great place to go.
All the children was happy and talk about the ponies and Sleepy Town.

When school was over the children run home so they soon talk to their grandmother and find out when they could go back to Sleepy Town. The children came running in the house.

"Where are you grandmother?"

"In the kitchen children," grandmother said.

"We would like to know more about Sleepy the pony. Please tell us all you know about him."

"Well children I will tell you he will come for you to night. And I will tell tonight at bed time."

They have their dinner and did their homework.

"Grandmother, we are ready for bed," said Billy.

"Ok, children I will be there." The grandmother walk into the room.

"Sleepy will come get you two soon."

The years pass by and it was Billy's birthday, he was turning twelve years old. It was time for the grandmother to tell Billy, he would not see Sleepy anymore.

"Billy it time for me to tell you. You would not remember Sleepy anymore till you become a grandfather with grandchildren of your own."

Billy looked at his at his grandmother. "Why is that grandmother?"

"Because that's the way it goes, Billy. When you have children, your parents will tell your children. And when your children have children you will tell them about Sleepy and his Town."

"Billy, you will not remember all the time that you were at Sleepy Town. Until your first—born grandchildren, turn 5 years old and then you may tell them about Sleepy and his town just I tell told you and Sara. Good night Billy."

Printed in the United States
by Baker & Taylor Publisher Services